TIME MANAGEMENT MASTERY:

Powerful Methods to Conquer Procrastination and Enhance Productivity

Victor T. Rice

DISCLAIMER

Copyright © Victor T. Rice 2024. All rights reserved.

Before this document is duplicated or reproduced in any manner, the publisher's consent must be gained. Therefore, the contents within can neither be stored electronically, transferred, nor kept in a database. Neither in Part nor full can the document be copied, scanned, faxed, or retained without approval from the publisher or creator.

Table of contents

Introduction: The Journey to Time Mastery 4

Chapter 1: The Psychology of Procrastination 6

Understanding the Procrastinator's Mindset 6

Common Causes and Triggers 7

Breaking the Cycle and overcoming procrastination 8

Chapter 2: How to Set Clear and realistic Goals 9

The Importance of Goal Setting 9

Develop your Action Plan with SMART goals aligned with your value? 12

Chapter 3: Prioritization Techniques 13

The Importance of Prioritization 13

Applying Prioritizing methods 14

Chapter 4: Time Blocking and Scheduling 16

How to Implement Time Blocking? 16

Creating a Functional Schedule 17

Chapter 5: Breaking Tasks into Manageable Steps ... 18

Why Breaking Tasks Down Works 18

Techniques for Breaking Down Tasks 19

Chapter 6: Enhance your focus and concentration to minimize distractions 21

The Importance of Focus and Concentration 21

Understanding Routines and Rituals 22

Understanding Resilience and Perseverance 24

Maintaining Motivation 27

Chapter 7: Advanced Scheduling Techniques and The Art of Saying No 29

Understanding Delegation and Outsourcing 30

Understanding the Importance of Saying No 33

Chapter 8: Work-Life Balance 36

Understanding Work-Life Balance 36

Strategies for Achieving Work-Life Balance 37

Conclusion 41

Introduction: The Journey to Time Mastery

Longed-for "Time Management Mastery: Powerful Methods to Conquer Procrastination and Enhance Productivity." If you've picked up this book, it's likely because you've experienced the frustration of procrastination and the desire to make the most of your time. You are not alone; procrastination is a challenge that affects millions of people, hindering personal growth, professional success, and overall well-being.

Why Time Management Matters

Time is our most valuable resource. Unlike money or possessions, once it's gone, we can never get it back. How we choose to spend our time directly impacts the quality of our lives, our relationships, and our achievements. Effective time management allows us to create a fulfilling and balanced life, where we can achieve our goals and enjoy our journey.

In today's fast-paced world, the demands on our time are greater than ever. We're constantly bombarded with information, tasks, and distractions, making it easy to feel overwhelmed and unproductive. This book is designed to help you take control of your time, reduce stress, and achieve more than you ever thought possible.

The Cost of Procrastination

Procrastination is more than just a bad habit; it's a significant barrier to success and happiness. It can lead to missed opportunities, increased stress, and a sense of guilt and inadequacy. When we procrastinate, we often delay important tasks, leading to rushed work, lower quality outcomes, and even failure to meet deadlines.

Procrastination isn't just about poor time management. It's a complex issue influenced by psychological, emotional, and environmental factors. Understanding these underlying causes is the first step towards overcoming procrastination and reclaiming your time.

What You Will Learn

"Time Management Mastery" is your comprehensive guide to conquering procrastination and enhancing your productivity. Throughout this book, you'll discover a variety of powerful methods and practical strategies to help you manage your time effectively. We'll explore:

- The psychology behind procrastination and how to break free from its grip.
- Techniques for setting clear, achievable goals and prioritizing your tasks.
- Practical strategies for scheduling, time blocking, and breaking tasks into manageable steps.
- Ways to enhance your focus to minimize distractions.
- The importance of routines, resilience, and maintaining motivation.
- Advanced time management techniques, including delegation and saying no.
- Integrating personal and professional life to achieve a balanced, fulfilling existence.

A Transformative Journey

Embarking on the journey to time mastery requires commitment and effort. It's not about universally applicable answers or fast fixes.

Instead, it's about making meaningful changes to your mindset, habits, and routines. This book will guide you through each step of the process, providing you with the tools and insights you need to succeed.

By the end of this book, you will have a deeper understanding of how to manage your time effectively and the confidence to implement these strategies in your daily life. You'll be equipped to overcome procrastination, achieve your goals, and create a more productive and fulfilling life.

Let's begin this journey together. Turn the page, and take the first step towards mastering your time and enhancing your productivity. Your future self will thank you.

Chapter 1: The Psychology of Procrastination

Procrastination is a complex and pervasive problem that affects nearly everyone at some point in their lives. It goes beyond simply putting off tasks; it's a habitual cycle that can have serious consequences for our personal and professional lives. In this chapter, we will delve into the psychology behind procrastination, exploring its causes, triggers, and the various ways it manifests.

Understanding the Procrastinator's Mindset

At its core, procrastination is often rooted in psychological factors. These can include fear of failure, perfectionism, low self-esteem, and a lack of motivation. Understanding these underlying causes is essential to breaking the cycle of procrastination.

Fear of Failure
To avoid failure is a common reason for procrastination.
 This fear can be paralyzing, leading them to avoid starting tasks altogether. The logic is simple: if you don't start, you can't fail. However, this mindset only serves to reinforce the fear and perpetuate procrastination.

Perfectionism
As a result of their impossible standards for themselves, perfectionists frequently put off tasks.
 The fear of not meeting these standards can lead to delaying tasks, as they wait for the "perfect" moment or the "perfect" conditions to begin. This pursuit of perfection can be a significant barrier to productivity.

Low Self-Esteem
Low self-esteem can also contribute to procrastination. When individuals doubt their abilities, they may avoid tasks to protect themselves from potential criticism

or judgment. This avoidance behavior can create a vicious cycle, where procrastination leads to further feelings of inadequacy.

Lack of Motivation
Motivation is a key driver of action. When motivation is low, tasks can seem overwhelming or unimportant, leading to procrastination. This lack of motivation can be caused by a variety of factors, including boredom, lack of interest, or not understanding the value of the task at hand.

Common Causes and Triggers

In addition to psychological factors, there are several common causes and triggers that can lead to procrastination. Identifying these can help you recognize when you are at risk of procrastinating and take steps to counteract it.

Immediate Gratification
The human brain is wired to seek immediate rewards and avoid discomfort. This is why tasks that offer immediate gratification, like checking social media or watching TV, can be so tempting. These activities provide a quick dopamine hit, making it difficult to focus on less immediately rewarding tasks.

Task Aversion
When a task is particularly unpleasant or challenging, it's natural to want to avoid it. This aversion can lead to procrastination as we seek to delay the discomfort associated with the task. The longer we avoid it, the more daunting it can seem, creating a cycle of avoidance.

Decision Fatigue
Making decisions requires mental energy. When we are faced with too many choices or decisions, it can lead to decision fatigue, where our ability to make decisions becomes impaired. This can result in procrastination as we put off making choices or taking action.

Overwhelm

Feeling overwhelmed by the sheer volume of tasks or the complexity of a particular task can also lead to procrastination. When we don't know where to start or feel that we can't handle everything on our plate, it's easy to become paralyzed and do nothing instead.

The Cycle of Procrastination
Procrastination often follows a predictable cycle. Recognizing this cycle can help you understand your patterns and take steps to break free from it.
1. **Delay**: You put off starting a task, often engaging in less important activities instead.
2. **Guilt**: As the deadline approaches, you start to feel guilty and stressed about not having started.
3. **Crisis**: The task becomes urgent, leading to a last-minute rush to complete it.
4. **Relief**: After completing the task, you feel a sense of relief, but the underlying issues remain unaddressed, setting the stage for the cycle to repeat.

Breaking the Cycle and overcoming procrastination

Understanding the psychology of procrastination is the first step towards breaking the cycle. The following techniques can assist you in overcoming procrastination:

- **Self-Reflection**: Take time to reflect on why you are procrastinating. Are you afraid of failure? Are you overwhelmed by the task? Understanding the underlying problem will allow you to successfully address it.

- **Set Realistic Goals:** Break down projects into smaller, more manageable chunks and set achievable goals for yourself. This can make activities appear less difficult and aid in the development of momentum.

- **Prioritize Tasks**: Use prioritization techniques, such as the Eisenhower Matrix, to identify and focus on the most important tasks.

- **Establish a Routine:** Make sure you have a regular schedule that includes time set out for concentrated work. Consistency can help reduce procrastination.

- **Breaking tasks into smaller:** Manageable steps is a powerful technique to overcome this feeling of overwhelm and make progress more achievable.

- **Practice Self-Compassion**: Be kind to yourself. Recognize that everyone procrastinates at times and that is a habit you can change with practice and persistence.

By understanding the psychological factors behind procrastination and implementing these strategies, you can begin to set realistic goals and break free from the cycle and take control of your time and productivity. These techniques will be discussed further in the following chapters.

Chapter 2: How to Set Clear and realistic Goals

The key to efficient time management is setting goals that are both specific and achievable.

Without well-defined goals, it's challenging to stay motivated, measure progress, and maintain focus. In this chapter, we'll explore the importance of goal setting, introduce the SMART goals framework, and discuss how to align your goals with your core values to ensure they are both meaningful and achievable.

The Importance of Goal Setting

Goals give direction and purpose to our efforts. They provide a roadmap for where we want to go and help us stay focused on what's important. Effective goal setting involves more than just stating what you want to achieve; it requires a thoughtful approach to ensure your goals are specific, attainable, and aligned with your long-term vision.

Benefits of Setting Goals

1. **Provides Clarity**: Clear goals help you understand what you need to do and what success looks like. Focus and anxiety levels can both be raised by this clarity.
2. **Increases Motivation**: Having goals gives you something to strive for, which can boost motivation and drive. The sense of purpose can make even challenging tasks more manageable.
3. **Enhances Performance**: Setting goals can improve performance by breaking down larger tasks into smaller, more manageable steps, making it easier to track progress and stay on course.
4. **Facilitates Planning**: Goals help you prioritize tasks and allocate resources effectively, ensuring that you focus your time and energy on what matters most.

The SMART Goals Framework

One of the most effective methods for setting clear and achievable goals is the SMART framework. SMART is an acronym that stands for Specific, Measurable, Achievable, Relevant, and Time-bound. Applying this framework can help you create goals that are well-defined and attainable.

S – Specific

What you aim to accomplish is made obvious with a precise goal. Questions like Who, What, Where, When, and Why are all addressed.

Specific goals provide clear direction and help you understand exactly what needs to be done.

- **Example**: Instead of setting a vague goal like "Improve my fitness," a specific goal would be "Attend a one-hour yoga class at the local studio three times a week."

M – Measurable

A measurable goal includes criteria to track progress and determine when the goal has been achieved. It answers the question: How much? How many? When it is completed, how will I know?

- **Example**: "Increase my sales by 20% within the next quarter" is a measurable goal because it includes a quantifiable target and a timeframe.

A – Achievable

A realistic and attainable goal is one that you can achieve within the limitations and resources you now have. It responds to the query: Is this objective feasible? It must be difficult, but it must also be attainable.

- **Example**: Setting a goal to "Read one book per month" is achievable for most people, whereas "Read 100 books in a month" may be unrealistic.

R- Relevant

A pertinent aim is consistent with your larger goals and principles. It provides an answer to the query, Does this objective matter to me? Make sure your objectives have purpose and advance your long-term objectives.

- **Example**: If your long-term career goal is to become a project manager, a relevant goal would be "Complete a project management certification course within the next six months."

T- Time-bound

A time-bound goal includes a deadline or timeframe for completion. It answers the question: When? By giving yourself a deadline, you can maintain concentration and foster a sense of urgency.

- **Example**: "Write and submit a research paper by December 31st" provides a clear deadline for completing the task.

Aligning Goals with Core Values

For goals to be truly effective, they need to resonate with your core values and long-term vision. Your likelihood of maintaining motivation and commitment to reaching your goals is higher when they are in line with your core values.

Identifying Core Values

Think about what matters most to you for a while.

Core values might include family, health, personal growth, financial stability, or community involvement. Understanding these values can help you set goals that are meaningful and fulfilling.

Aligning Goals with Values

Once you have identified your core values, ensure that your goals align with them. For example, if health is a core value, setting a goal to "Incorporate a healthy diet and exercise routine into my daily life" aligns with this value and supports your overall well-being.

Develop your Action Plan with SMART goals aligned with your value?

With your SMART goals in place and aligned with your values, it's time to develop an action plan. This plan should outline the specific steps you need to take to achieve your goals, including:

1. **Breaking Down Goals**: Assign more difficult objectives to smaller, more doable activities. They become easier to handle and less intimidating as a result.
2. **Creating a Timeline**: Establish a timeline for completing each task and reaching your goal. This helps you stay organized and track progress.
3. **Identifying Resources**: Determine what resources, tools, or support you need to achieve your goals. This might include additional training, financial investment, or guidance from a mentor.
4. **Monitoring Progress**: Regularly review your progress towards your goals and adjust your action plan as needed. Celebrate milestones and make any necessary changes to stay on track.

Setting clear and achievable goals is a critical component of effective time management. By applying the SMART framework and aligning your goals with your core values, you can create a roadmap for success that motivates you and guides your efforts. In the next chapter, we will explore prioritization techniques to help you focus on what matters most and make the most of your time.

Chapter 3: Prioritization Techniques

Effective prioritization is key to managing your time efficiently and ensuring that your efforts are directed toward what truly matters. In this chapter, we will explore various prioritization techniques to help you identify and focus on your most important tasks. By mastering these techniques, you can make better decisions about where to invest your time and energy, ultimately leading to increased productivity and satisfaction.

The Importance of Prioritization

Setting priorities entails arranging tasks in accordance with their urgency and significance.

Proper prioritization helps you focus on high-impact activities, avoid getting bogged down by less critical tasks, and ensure that you are making progress toward your goals. Without effective prioritization, it's easy to become overwhelmed, distracted, and less productive.

Benefits of Prioritizing Tasks

1. **Improves Focus**: By focusing on high-priority tasks, you can direct your attention and energy to activities that contribute most to your goals.
2. **Enhances Efficiency**: Prioritization helps you work more efficiently by avoiding time spent on less important or low-impact tasks.
3. **Reduces Stress**: Knowing what tasks are most important and addressing them first can reduce feelings of overwhelm and stress.
4. **Increases Achievement**: Prioritizing tasks allows you to make steady progress toward your goals and achieve more in less time.

Applying Prioritizing methods

The Eisenhower Matrix
The Urgent-Important Matrix, sometimes referred to as the Eisenhower Matrix, is a widely used method for setting work priorities according to their urgency and significance. You can divide tasks into four quadrants with the aid of this matrix:

(Quadrant I)
1. **Urgent and Important**: Tasks in this quadrant require immediate attention and have significant consequences. Priority should be given to them.
    - **Example**: An impending project deadline or a critical client issue.

(Quadrant II)

2. **Important but Not Urgent:** Activities in this quadrant don't need to be completed right now, but they are necessary to reach your long-term objectives. It is necessary to schedule and plan these tasks.
    - **Example**: Strategic planning, personal development, or relationship-building activities.

(Quadrant III)

3. **Urgent but Not Important**: Tasks in this quadrant require immediate attention but are not critical to your long-term goals. These tasks can often be delegated or minimized.
    a. **Example**: Interruptions or routine requests that do not align with your core objectives.

(Quadrant IV)

4. **Not Urgent and Not Important**: Tasks in this quadrant have little value and do not contribute to your goals. One should reduce or do away with these tasks.

a. **Example**: Time-wasting activities or excessive social media browsing.

The Pareto Principle (80/20 Rule)

The 80/20 Rule, sometimes referred to as the Pareto Principle, states that 20% of your efforts provide 80% of the results.

This principle emphasizes the importance of focusing on the few tasks that have the greatest impact on your outcomes.

Applying the Pareto Principle

1. **Identify High-Impact Tasks**: Determine which tasks or activities contribute the most to your goals and results. These are the tasks that should receive the majority of your attention.
2. **Eliminate or Delegate Low-Impact Tasks**: Reduce or delegate tasks that do not significantly contribute to your goals. This helps free up time for more important activities.
3. **Review and Adjust**: Regularly assess your tasks and activities to ensure that you are focusing on the most impactful areas.

The ABCDE Method

The ABCDE Method is a prioritization technique that involves categorizing tasks based on their level of importance. Each task is assigned a letter from A to E, with A being the highest priority and E being the lowest.

1. **A - Most Important**: Tasks that are critical to your goals and must be completed as soon as possible.
    - **Example**: Completing a major report for a key client.
2. **B - Important**: Tasks that are important but not as urgent as A tasks. They should be addressed after A tasks are completed.
    - **Example**: Preparing for a team meeting or reviewing a draft proposal.
3. **C - Nice to Do**: Tasks that are neither urgent nor critical. They can be completed if time allows but should not take precedence over A or B tasks.

- **Example**: Organizing your workspace or attending a networking event.
4. **D - Delegate**: Tasks that can be delegated to others. This helps you focus on tasks that require your specific expertise.
    - **Example**: Assigning routine administrative tasks to a team member.
5. **E - Eliminate**: Tasks that are unnecessary and do not contribute to your goals. These should be eliminated to avoid wasting time.
    - **Example**: Attending meetings that do not provide value or engaging in non-productive activities.

Prioritization is a crucial skill for effective time management. By using techniques such as the Eisenhower Matrix, the Pareto Principle, the ABCDE Method, and time blocking, you can focus on the tasks that matter most, enhance your productivity, and achieve your goals more efficiently. In the next chapter, we will explore how to use time blocking and scheduling and making them less overwhelming and easier to tackle.

Chapter 4: Time Blocking and Scheduling

Effective time management is not just about setting goals and prioritizing tasks; it also involves creating a structured schedule that allows you to allocate your time wisely. Time blocking and scheduling are powerful techniques for managing your time more effectively, ensuring that you stay focused and productive throughout the day. In this chapter, we'll explore how to implement time blocking, create a functional schedule, and make the most of your time.

What is Time Blocking?

Time blocking is a scheduling technique where you divide your day into specific blocks of time, each dedicated to a particular task or activity. This approach helps you stay organized, minimize distractions, and make steady progress on your goals.

Benefits of Time Blocking

1. **Improved Focus**: Time blocking allows you to concentrate on one task at a time, reducing the likelihood of multitasking and improving overall focus.

2. **Enhanced Productivity**: By allocating dedicated time for specific tasks, you can make more efficient use of your time and achieve better results.

3. **Reduced Stress**: Having a clear plan for your day can help you manage your workload more effectively, reducing feelings of overwhelm and stress.

4. **Better Time Management**: Time blocking makes it easier to spot and fix inefficiencies by allowing you to see how your time is spent.

How to Implement Time Blocking?

1. **Identify Key Tasks and Activities**: Start by listing all the tasks and activities you need to complete. Include work-related tasks, meetings, personal commitments, and any other responsibilities.

2. **Estimate Time Requirements**: Estimate how much time each task or activity will take. Be realistic and consider factors such as breaks and potential interruptions.

3. **Create Time Blocks**: Divide your day into time blocks based on your estimates. Set up specified time slots for every task or activity.
   - For example, you might set aside 9:00 AM - 10:30 AM for project work, 10:30 AM - 11:00 AM for email, and 11:00 AM - 12:00 PM for a team meeting.

4. **Schedule Breaks and Downtime**: Include time blocks for breaks, meals, and relaxation. Regular breaks might assist you in staying focused and preventing burnout.

5. **Use a Calendar or Planner**: Record your time blocks in a calendar or planner. Digital tools, such as Google Calendar or Outlook, can be especially useful for setting reminders and keeping track of your schedule.

6. **Stick to the Plan**: Follow your time blocks as closely as possible. Reduce outside distractions as much as possible and maintain concentration during each block. Just modify your timetable to account for unforeseen chores or disruptions.

Creating a Functional Schedule

A well-designed schedule helps you organize your day, manage your time effectively, and ensure that you stay on track with your goals. The following advice can help you make a timetable or schedule that works:

Prioritize Your Tasks: Ensure that your schedule reflects your priorities. Focus on high-impact tasks and allocate sufficient time for activities that are critical to achieving your goals. Use the prioritization techniques discussed in Chapter 3 to guide your scheduling decisions.

Plan Your Day: Start by planning your day the evening before or first thing in the morning. Review your to-do list, set your priorities, and create a schedule that outlines when and how you will complete each task.

Allocate Time for Strategic Planning: Include time blocks for strategic planning and reflection in your schedule. Regularly review your progress, adjust your goals, and plan for the future. This helps you stay aligned with your long-term objectives and ensures that you are making steady progress.

Be Flexible and Adaptable: While time blocking and scheduling are essential for effective time management, it's important to remain flexible. Life is unpredictable, and unexpected events or changes in priorities may require adjustments to your schedule. Be willing to adjust and make changes as necessary.

Time blocking and scheduling are powerful techniques for managing your time more effectively. By creating a structured plan for your day and allocating dedicated time for each task, you can improve your focus, enhance productivity, and reduce stress. In the next chapter, we will explore how to break tasks into manageable steps, making them less overwhelming and easier to tackle.

Chapter 5: Breaking Tasks into Manageable Steps

One of the most common reasons people procrastinate is that they feel overwhelmed by the size or complexity of a task. Breaking tasks into smaller, manageable steps is a powerful technique to overcome this feeling of overwhelm and make progress more achievable. In this chapter, we'll explore various methods for breaking down tasks, the benefits of this approach, and practical strategies to implement it effectively.

Why Breaking Tasks Down Works

Large tasks or projects can seem daunting and unmanageable, leading to procrastination or avoidance. Breaking tasks into smaller steps can make them seem more approachable and less intimidating. This technique helps by:

1. **Reducing Overwhelm**: Smaller tasks feel more manageable and less overwhelming than large, complex projects. Starting and keeping momentum may be much simpler as a result.

2. **Providing Clear Direction**: Each step outlines a specific action to take, providing clear direction and reducing ambiguity about what needs to be done.

3. **Enhancing Motivation**: Completing smaller tasks can provide a sense of accomplishment and progress, boosting motivation and making it easier to tackle the next step.

4. **Facilitating Planning**: Breaking tasks down allows you to plan more effectively and allocate time and resources appropriately.

Steps to Break Down Tasks

1. **Define the End Goal**: Start by clearly defining the overall goal or outcome you want to achieve. Understand what the final result looks like and what success means for this task or project.
   - **Example**: If your goal is to write a research paper, the result is a completed, polished paper ready for submission.

2. **Identify Major Components**: Break the end goal into major components or phases. These are the broad areas or sections that need to be addressed to achieve the final result.
   - **Example**: For a research paper, major components might include research, outlining, writing, and editing.

3. **Break Components into Subtasks**: Further divide each major component into smaller, actionable subtasks. These subtasks should be specific, manageable, and have clear outcomes.
   - **Example**:
     - **Research**: Identify research sources, gather articles, and summarize key findings.
     - **Outlining**: Create an outline, organize the main points, and develop a thesis statement.
     - **Writing**: Write the introduction, develop body paragraphs, and draft the conclusion.
     - **Editing**: Review for grammar, check citations, and format the document.

4. **Set Milestones**: Establish milestones to track progress and celebrate achievements. Milestones are key points or achievements within the project that help you monitor progress and stay motivated.

- **Example**: Completing the research phase or finishing the first draft of the paper.
5. **Create a Timeline**: Develop a timeline for completing each subtask and milestone. Allocate specific time blocks for working on each task and set deadlines to keep yourself on track.

    - **Example**: Schedule time for research over the next two weeks, outline the paper by the end of the month, and complete the first draft within four weeks.

Techniques for Breaking Down Tasks

1. The Two-Minute Rule

According to the Two-Minute Rule, you should accomplish a task right away if it can be finished in two minutes or less.
For larger tasks, break them down into subtasks that can be completed in a few minutes each. This technique helps you start working on tasks and makes progress feel more manageable.

- **Example**: If you need to respond to an email, and it will take less than two minutes, handle it right away. For a larger project, identify subtasks that can be completed quickly and address them as part of the overall process.

2. Mind Mapping

Mind mapping is a visual technique for breaking down tasks and organizing ideas. Create a central node for the main goal and branch out into major components and subtasks. This visual representation helps you see the connections between tasks and organize them more effectively.

- **Example**: Start with a central node labeled "Research Paper" and create branches for research, outlining, writing, and editing. Further branch out each major component into specific subtasks.

3. Task Hierarchies

Task hierarchies involve organizing tasks into a hierarchical structure, with the main goal at the top and subtasks arranged below. This approach helps you see the relationship between tasks and understand the order in which they should be completed.

- **Example**:
    - **Main Goal**: Submit Research Paper
    - **Research**: Gather Sources, Summarize Findings
    - **Outline**: Create Outline, Develop Thesis
    - **Writing**: Draft Introduction, Write Body, Conclude
    - **Editing**: Proofread, Format, Cite Sources

Implementing the Approach

1. **Use Tools and Templates**: Utilize tools such as to-do lists, project management software, or templates to help you organize and track your tasks. Tools like Trello, Asana, or even simple spreadsheets can be effective.

2. **Review and Adjust**: Regularly review your progress and adjust your task breakdown as needed. If you encounter obstacles or changes, update your tasks and timeline accordingly.

3. **Celebrate Progress**: Acknowledge and celebrate the completion of subtasks and milestones. This helps maintain motivation and reinforces the sense of accomplishment.

Breaking tasks into manageable steps is a powerful technique for overcoming procrastination and achieving your goals. By defining clear steps, setting milestones, and using practical techniques like the Two-Minute Rule, mind mapping, and task hierarchies, you can make large tasks feel more achievable and maintain steady progress. In the next chapter, we will explore strategies for enhancing focus and concentration, routines and rituals, resilience and perseverance, maintaining motivation, helping you stay on track and maximize your productivity.

Chapter 6: Enhance your focus and concentration to minimize distractions

The Importance of Focus and Concentration

Focus and concentration are crucial for productivity and achieving high-quality results. When you can concentrate on a single task, you complete it more efficiently and effectively. Enhanced focus leads to better decision-making, fewer mistakes, and higher satisfaction with your work.

Benefits of Improved Focus
1. **Increased Productivity**: By concentrating on one task at a time, you can complete tasks more quickly and efficiently.
2. **Higher Quality Work**: Focused work leads to fewer errors and higher-quality outcomes.
3. **Reduced Stress**: Improved concentration can reduce the stress associated with multitasking and incomplete tasks.
4. **Greater Satisfaction**: Achieving your goals with focused effort can lead to a greater sense of accomplishment and satisfaction.

Tools and Techniques for Better Focus

1. **Focus Apps and Tools**

Several apps and tools can help you stay focused and manage distractions.
- Focus@Will: Provides background music meant to improve attention.
- **Forest**: Encourages focus by growing a virtual tree while you work and discourages phone use.
- **Freedom**: Blocks distracting websites and apps to help you stay on task.

2. **Task Management Software**

Task management software can help you organize and prioritize tasks, reducing the likelihood of feeling overwhelmed.
- **Todoist**: A task management app that allows you to create, prioritize, and track tasks.

- Trello is a visual project management application for organizing tasks and collaborating with colleagues.

3. **Time Tracking Tools**

Time tracking tools can help you keep track of how you spend your time and find opportunities for development.

- **Toggle**: Tracks time spent on tasks and projects, providing insights into your work habits.
- **RescueTime**: Monitors your computer usage to help you identify and address distractions.

Understanding Routines and Rituals

1. **Defining Routines**

Routines are regular, repeated activities that you perform in a specific sequence. They help create structure and predictability in your daily life, allowing you to manage your time more effectively.

- **Daily Routines**: Activities performed daily, such as morning and evening routines, which set the tone for your day.
- **Work Routines**: Consistent practices and procedures that guide your work tasks and productivity.

2. **Defining Rituals**

Rituals are meaningful practices that often have personal or cultural significance. They can be used to mark transitions, celebrate achievements, or provide a sense of purpose and connection.

- **Personal Rituals**: Activities that have personal significance and contribute to your well-being, such as meditation or journaling.
- **Work Rituals**: Practices that help you transition into work mode or enhance your work environment, such as a pre-work routine or closing ritual.

The Benefits of Routines and Rituals

1. **Increased Efficiency**

Routines and rituals help streamline your activities and reduce the need for constant decision-making, leading to greater efficiency.

- **Automate Tasks**: Routine tasks become automatic, freeing up cognitive resources for more complex tasks.
- **Reduce Decision Fatigue**: Consistent routines minimize the need to make decisions about routine activities, reducing mental fatigue.

2. **Enhanced Focus**

Well-established routines and rituals can improve focus by creating a structured environment and reducing distractions.

- **Signal Transitions**: Rituals can signal transitions between activities, helping you mentally shift focus and stay on track.
- **Create a Productive Environment**: Routines help maintain an organized workspace and minimize interruptions.

3. **Improved Well-Being**

Consistent routines and meaningful rituals contribute to overall well-being by promoting stability, reducing stress, and fostering a sense of purpose.

- **Build Positive Habits**: Regular routines support the development of positive habits and self-discipline.
- **Enhance Emotional Health**: Rituals provide opportunities for reflection, celebration, and personal fulfillment.

Creating Effective Routines

1. **Identify Key Areas**

Start by identifying the key areas of your life where routines can have the most impact. Focus on daily routines that set the stage for a productive day and work routines that enhance your efficiency.

- **Morning Routine**: Establish a morning routine that prepares you for the day ahead, such as exercise, breakfast, and planning.

- **Work Routine**: Develop a work routine that includes planning, task prioritization, and regular breaks.

2. **Design Your Routine**

Create a routine that aligns with your goals and preferences. Consider your daily schedule, energy levels, and priorities when designing your routine.

- **Start with Core Activities**: Include essential activities in your routine, such as exercise, meal preparation, and work tasks.
- **Add Personal Touches**: Incorporate elements that are personally meaningful or enjoyable to make the routine more engaging.

3. **Implement Gradually**

Introduce new routines gradually to avoid overwhelming yourself. Start with one or two key activities and build upon them over time.

- **Begin with Small Changes**: Start with small, manageable changes and gradually expand your routine.
- **Monitor and Adjust**: Observe how the routine affects your productivity and well-being, and make adjustments as needed.

Understanding Resilience and Perseverance

Defining Resilience

Resilience is the capacity to overcome obstacles, adjust to change, and keep a positive attitude in the face of hardship.

. It involves emotional strength, adaptability, and the capacity to recover from difficulties.

- **Emotional Strength**: The ability to manage stress and maintain emotional stability during challenging times.
- **Adaptability**: The capacity to adjust to new situations and changes in circumstances.
- **Recovery**: The ability to rebound from setbacks and continue moving forward.

Defining Perseverance

Perseverance is the persistence and determination to continue working towards your goals despite obstacles and challenges. It involves maintaining focus, staying motivated, and not giving up in the face of difficulties.

- **Persistence**: The commitment to keep going despite setbacks and obstacles.
- **Determination**: The drive to achieve goals and overcome challenges.
- **Long-Term Focus**: The ability to stay focused on long-term objectives despite short-term difficulties.

Building Resilience

1. **Cultivate a Growth Mindset**

A growth mindset helps you view challenges as opportunities for learning and growth. Embrace the belief that abilities and intelligence can be developed through effort and persistence.

- **Embrace Challenges**: View challenges as opportunities to learn and improve.
- **Learn from Failures**: Analyze failures and setbacks to gain insights and make improvements.

2. **Develop Emotional Awareness**

Emotional awareness involves understanding and managing your emotions effectively. Recognize your emotional responses to challenges and develop strategies to manage them.

- **Practice Self-Reflection**: Regularly reflect on your emotional responses and triggers.
- **Use Coping Strategies**: Implement coping strategies, such as mindfulness or journaling, to manage stress and emotions.

3. **Build Support Networks**

Surround yourself with supportive individuals who can provide encouragement, advice, and perspective during challenging times.

- **Seek Mentors and Allies**: Connect with mentors or colleagues who can offer guidance and support.
- **Foster Positive Relationships**: Build and maintain relationships with friends and family who provide emotional support.

4. **Set Realistic Goals**

Establish realistic and achievable goals that align with your values and priorities. To make development more achievable, break down big goals into smaller, more doable steps.

- **Define Clear Objectives**: Set specific and measurable goals that provide direction and motivation.
- **Create Action Plans**: Develop action plans to outline the steps needed to achieve your goals.

5. **Practice Self-Care**

Maintaining your physical and mental health is essential to developing resilience. Incorporate self-care practices into your routine to maintain overall health and balance.

- **Prioritize Health**: Focus on maintaining a healthy lifestyle through regular exercise, balanced nutrition, and adequate sleep.
- **Engage in Relaxation**: Practice relaxation techniques, such as meditation or deep breathing, to manage stress.

Fostering Perseverance

1. **Maintain a Long-Term Vision**

Having a clear long-term vision helps you stay focused and motivated, even when facing short-term challenges. Keep your overarching goals in mind to maintain perspective and direction.

- **Visualize Success**: Regularly visualize your long-term goals and the steps needed to achieve them.
- **Revisit Your Vision**: Periodically review and reaffirm your long-term vision to stay motivated.

2. **Stay Motivated**

Find and nurture sources of motivation that drive you towards your goals. Use intrinsic and extrinsic motivators to maintain enthusiasm and commitment.

- **Identify Motivators**: Determine what motivates you, such as personal passion, rewards, or recognition.
- **Celebrate Progress**: Recognize and celebrate milestones and achievements to maintain motivation.

3. **Develop Problem-Solving Skills**

Strong problem-solving skills help you navigate obstacles and find solutions to challenges. Enhance your ability to address problems effectively.

- **Analyze Challenges**: Break down challenges into manageable components and develop strategies to address them.
- **Seek Creative Solutions**: Approach problems with creativity and explore alternative solutions.

4. **Build Persistence Through Practice**

Practice persistence by tackling small challenges and gradually increasing the difficulty. Building persistence through practice helps develop a resilient mindset.

- **Set Incremental Challenges**: Start with smaller challenges and progressively take on more difficult tasks.
- **Learn from Experience**: Use past experiences to build confidence and perseverance.

5. **Embrace Flexibility**

Flexibility allows you to adapt your strategies and approach when faced with unexpected challenges. Be willing to adjust your strategies and plans as necessary.

Adjust Goals: Be willing to adjust your goals and action plans in response to changing circumstances.

- **Stay Adaptable**: Cultivate the ability to adapt to new situations and requirements.

Maintaining Motivation

1. **Stay Engaged**

Keep yourself engaged and motivated by periodically reviewing and updating your routines and rituals. Introduce new elements to maintain interest and enthusiasm.

- **Incorporate Variety**: Add new activities or variations to your routines and rituals to keep them fresh and engaging.
- **Celebrate Achievements**: Recognize and celebrate your progress and accomplishments to maintain motivation.

2. **Reflect on Benefits**

Regularly reflect on the benefits and positive impact of your routines and rituals. Remind yourself of the value they bring to your life and productivity.

- **Track Improvements**: Note the improvements in productivity and well-being resulting from your routines and rituals.
- **Reinforce Positive Outcomes**: Use the positive outcomes as motivation to continue and enhance your practices.

Developing resilience and perseverance is crucial for achieving long-term success and overcoming challenges. By cultivating a growth mindset, building support networks, maintaining motivation, and practicing self-care, you can strengthen your ability to navigate difficulties and stay committed to your goals. Implement these strategies to build resilience and perseverance, ensuring that you maintain momentum and achieve lasting success. In the final chapter, we'll explore how to advanced scheduling techniques and the art of saying no throughout for continued productivity and personal growth.

Chapter 7: Advanced Scheduling Techniques and The Art of Saying No

Mastering the art of saying "no" is essential for managing your time effectively, maintaining boundaries, and focusing on what truly matters. While it may seem difficult, saying "no" is a crucial skill for preventing over commitment, reducing stress, and achieving your goals. In this chapter, we will explore the importance of saying "no," strategies for doing so effectively, and the benefits it brings to your productivity and well-being.

In addition to basic time blocking, there are several advanced scheduling techniques that can further enhance your time management:

The Pomodoro Technique

Working in focused periods, usually 25 minutes long, followed by a 5-minute rest, is known as the Pomodoro Technique.

After completing four intervals, you take a longer break of 15-30 minutes. This technique helps improve focus and productivity by breaking work into manageable chunks and incorporating regular breaks.

Time Blocking with Buffer Time

Incorporate buffer time between your time blocks to account for unexpected interruptions or overruns. This additional time helps ensure that you stay on track and can handle any unforeseen issues that arise.

Thematic Days

Thematic days involve dedicating entire days or blocks of time to specific types of tasks or projects. For example, you might designate Mondays for administrative tasks, Tuesdays for client meetings, and Wednesdays for project work. This approach helps you focus on related activities and reduces the cognitive load of switching between different types of tasks.

Understanding Delegation and Outsourcing

1. **Defining Delegation**

   Delegation involves assigning tasks and responsibilities to others, typically within an organization or team. It allows you to distribute work, focus on high-priority tasks, and develop the skills of team members.

   - **Internal Delegation**: Assigning tasks to team members or colleagues within your organization.
   - **Task Distribution**: Allocating specific tasks or projects based on individual skills and expertise.

2. **Defining Outsourcing**

   Outsourcing refers to contracting external individuals or organizations to perform tasks or services that are typically handled in-house. It can be used to access specialized skills, reduce costs, or manage workload.

   - **External Providers**: Engaging third-party services or freelancers to complete specific tasks or projects.
   - **Cost and Efficiency**: Using outsourcing to reduce operational costs and improve efficiency.

Benefits of Delegation and Outsourcing

1. **Enhanced Productivity**

   Delegation and outsourcing can significantly increase productivity by allowing you to focus on high-priority tasks and strategic goals.

   - **Focus on Core Activities**: Allocate more time to activities that align with your strengths and strategic objectives.

- **Streamline Processes**: Delegate or outsource routine tasks to streamline operations and improve overall efficiency.

2. Access to Expertise

By delegating or outsourcing tasks, you gain access to specialized skills and knowledge that may not be available in-house.

- **Leverage Skills**: Utilize the expertise of team members or external providers to achieve higher-quality results.
- **Innovative Solutions**: Benefit from fresh perspectives and innovative approaches brought by external professionals.

3. Cost Savings

Outsourcing can lead to cost savings by reducing the need for additional staff or resources.

- **Reduce Overhead Costs**: Outsource non-core functions to minimize overhead and operational expenses.
- **Scalable Solutions**: Use outsourcing to scale resources up or down based on project needs and budget.

4. Improved Time Management

Delegation and outsourcing help you manage your time more effectively by redistributing tasks and responsibilities.

- **Prioritize Tasks**: Focus on high-impact tasks while delegating or outsourcing lower-priority activities.
- **Free Up Time**: Allocate time to strategic activities and personal development by offloading routine tasks.

Effective Delegation Strategies

1. Identify Tasks to Delegate

Determine which tasks are suitable for delegation based on their complexity, importance, and the skills required.

- **Assess Task Complexity**: Delegate tasks that are manageable and align with the skills of the person you're delegating to.
- **Evaluate Impact**: Consider the impact of the task on overall goals and objectives when deciding whether to delegate.

2. **Select the Right Person**

Choose individuals who have the appropriate skills, experience, and capacity to handle the delegated tasks effectively.

- **Match Skills to Tasks**: Assign tasks based on the strengths and expertise of team members.
- **Consider Availability**: Ensure that the person you delegate to has the time and resources to complete the task.

3. **Communicate Clearly**

Provide clear instructions and expectations when delegating tasks. Effective communication helps ensure that the task is completed as intended.

- **Define Objectives**: Clearly outline the goals, objectives, and desired outcomes of the task.
- **Provide Resources**: Supply any necessary resources, tools, or information needed to complete the task.

4. **Monitor and Support**

Monitor progress and provide support as needed to ensure that the task is completed successfully.

- **Check-In Regularly**: Schedule regular check-ins to review progress and address any issues or questions.
- **Offer Guidance**: Provide feedback and guidance to help overcome challenges and achieve the desired results.
-

5. **Acknowledge and Appreciate**

Recognize and appreciate the efforts of those who take on delegated tasks. Positive reinforcement encourages continued engagement and performance.

- **Provide Feedback**: Offer constructive feedback and acknowledge accomplishments.
- **Show Appreciation**: Express gratitude for the work completed and the contribution to overall success.

Understanding the Importance of Saying No

1. Preventing Over commitment

Saying "no" helps prevent taking on too many responsibilities and commitments, which can lead to overwhelm and decreased productivity.

- **Avoiding Burnout**: By turning down additional tasks or commitments, you reduce the risk of burnout and stress.
- **Managing Workload**: Maintain a manageable workload by focusing on existing responsibilities and priorities.

2. Maintaining Boundaries

Setting and maintaining boundaries is crucial for balancing personal and professional life. "No" helps you save time and energy.

Protecting Personal Time: Preserve time for personal activities and relaxation by declining non-essential requests.

- **Establishing Professional Limits**: Define limits on work-related tasks to prevent encroachment on personal time and well-being.

3. Focusing on Priorities

Saying "no" allows you to concentrate on your most important goals and priorities, enhancing your overall effectiveness and success.

- **Aligning with Goals**: Ensure that your efforts are aligned with your key objectives by avoiding distractions and unrelated tasks.
- **Enhancing Productivity**: Focus on high-impact activities and projects that contribute to your long-term success.

Strategies for Saying No Effectively

1. **Be Clear and Direct**

   When saying "no," be clear, direct, and concise. Avoid ambiguity or uncertainty in your response.

   - **Use Simple Language**: Communicate your refusal clearly using straightforward language.
   - **Be Assertive**: Stand firm in your decision without over-explaining or justifying.

2. **Offer Alternatives**

   If appropriate, offer alternative solutions or suggestions when declining a request. This can help maintain positive relationships and provide support.

   - **Suggest Alternatives**: Propose other options or resources that may help the requester.
   - **Recommend Colleagues**: Refer them to someone else who may be able to assist with their request.

3. **Use the "Sandwich" Approach**

   The "sandwich" approach involves framing your refusal with positive statements. This method helps soften the impact and maintains goodwill.

   - **Start with Positivity**: Begin with a positive or appreciative statement.
   - **State Your Refusal**: Clearly communicate your inability to fulfill the request.
   - **End with Encouragement**: Conclude with a supportive or encouraging comment.

4. **Practice Empathy**

   Show understanding and empathy towards the requester, even when declining their request. This approach helps preserve relationships and demonstrates consideration.

- **Acknowledge Their Situation**: Recognize the importance of their request and express empathy for their needs.
- **Express Regret**: Show genuine regret for not being able to assist while maintaining your boundaries.

5. **Be Honest and Transparent**

Honesty is key when saying "no." Provide truthful reasons for your decision without oversharing personal details.

- **Explain Briefly**: Offer a brief explanation for your refusal if appropriate, but avoid excessive details.
- **Be Authentic**: Communicate your decision authentically and respectfully.

The Benefits of Saying No

1. **Improved Focus and Productivity**

Saying "no" allows you to concentrate on your most important tasks and goals, leading to enhanced productivity and effectiveness.

- **Reduce Distractions**: Minimize interruptions and distractions by focusing on your priorities.
- **Increase Efficiency**: Allocate more time and energy to high-impact activities.

2. **Enhanced Well-Being**

Setting boundaries and managing commitments helps reduce stress and improve overall well-being.

- **Prevent Burnout**: Avoid overcommitting and protect your mental and physical health.
- **Maintain Balance**: Achieve a better balance between work and personal life.

3. **Strengthened Relationships**

   Saying "no" with empathy and respect helps maintain positive relationships while protecting your own needs and boundaries.

   - **Build Trust**: Demonstrate reliability and integrity by managing your commitments effectively.
   - **Foster Respect**: Cultivate mutual respect by setting clear boundaries and communicating honestly.
   -

Mastering the art of saying "no" is essential for managing your time, maintaining boundaries, and focusing on your priorities. By being clear, direct, and empathetic, you can decline requests effectively while preserving positive relationships. Overcoming challenges such as guilt and pushback, and understanding the benefits of setting boundaries, will help you achieve greater productivity, well-being, and success. Embrace the power of saying "no" as a valuable tool for achieving your goals and maintaining balance in your life.

Chapter 8: Work-Life Balance

Achieving a harmonious work-life balance is essential for maintaining overall well-being, enhancing productivity, and leading a fulfilling life. Balancing the demands of work with personal responsibilities and interests can be challenging, but with intentional strategies and practices, it is possible to create a sustainable and rewarding balance. In this chapter, we will explore the principles of work-life balance, strategies for achieving it, and the benefits it brings to your personal and professional life.

Understanding Work-Life Balance

1. **Defining Work-Life Balance**

When work and personal life are balanced, there is an equal amount of time and energy dedicated to each.

It involves managing the demands of your job while ensuring time for family, hobbies, relaxation, and self-care.

- **Equilibrium**: Striving for a balanced distribution of time and effort between work and personal life.
- **Integration**: Harmonizing work responsibilities with personal interests and relationships.

2. **The Importance of Work-Life Balance**

Maintaining work-life balance is crucial for overall well-being and success. It impacts physical health, mental health, relationships, and job satisfaction.

- **Health and Well-Being**: Preventing burnout and stress by managing work demands and personal time.
- **Relationship Quality**: Enhancing relationships with family and friends by dedicating time to personal life.
- **Job Satisfaction**: Improving job satisfaction and performance by achieving a healthy balance.

Strategies for Achieving Work-Life Balance

1. **Set Clear Boundaries**

Establishing clear boundaries between work and personal life helps prevent overlap and ensures dedicated time for each area.

- **Define Work Hours**: Set specific work hours and avoid working beyond these times.
- **Create a Dedicated Workspace**: Designate a specific area for work to separate it from personal spaces.

2. **Prioritize and Plan**

Prioritizing tasks and planning your time effectively allows you to manage both work and personal responsibilities more efficiently.

- **Identify Priorities**: Determine your key priorities for both work and personal life.
- **Use Time Management Tools**: Utilize tools such as calendars, planners, and to-do lists to organize and plan your tasks.

3. **Learn to Delegate**

Delegating tasks at work and at home can help manage your workload and free up time for personal activities.

- **Delegate at Work**: Assign tasks to colleagues or team members to distribute workload effectively.
- **Share Household Responsibilities**: Involve family members in managing household chores and responsibilities.

4. **Practice Self-Care**

Taking care of your physical, emotional, and mental health is essential for maintaining balance and overall well-being.

- **Regular Exercise**: Incorporate physical activity into your routine to boost energy and reduce stress.

- **Healthy Eating**: Maintain a balanced diet to support physical and mental health.
- **Relaxation and Hobbies**: Engage in activities that you enjoy and that help you relax.

5. **Manage Stress**

Developing effective stress management techniques helps maintain balance and prevent burnout.

- **Stress-Reduction Techniques**: Practice techniques such as meditation, deep breathing, or mindfulness.
- **Seek Support**: Reach out for support from friends, family, or professionals when needed.

6. **Communicate Effectively**

Open and honest communication with your employer, colleagues, and family helps manage expectations and ensure support.

- **Discuss Boundaries**: Communicate your work and personal boundaries with your employer and family.
- **Request Flexibility**: Seek flexible work arrangements if necessary to better balance work and personal life.

Overcoming Common Challenges

1. **Managing Work Demands**

Balancing demanding work responsibilities with personal life can be challenging. Implement strategies to manage work demands effectively.

- **Set Realistic Goals**: Set achievable goals and avoid overcommitting to tasks or projects.
- **Use Time Blocking**: Allocate specific time blocks for work and personal activities to ensure focus and balance.

2. **Handling Work-Related Stress**

Work-related stress can impact work-life balance. Develop strategies to manage stress and maintain balance.

- **Practice Stress Management**: Implement stress management techniques to cope with work-related pressures.
- **Take Breaks**: Incorporate regular breaks into your workday to reduce stress and maintain productivity.

3. **Balancing Family Responsibilities**

Managing family responsibilities alongside work can be challenging. Develop strategies to balance family needs with professional obligations.

- **Share Responsibilities**: Collaborate with family members to share household and caregiving responsibilities.
- **Schedule Family Time**: Plan and prioritize quality time with family to strengthen relationships and balance responsibilities.

4. **Avoiding Perfectionism**

Striving for perfection can lead to overwork and imbalance. Embrace a balanced approach and avoid setting unrealistic expectations.

- **Set Realistic Standards**: Accept that perfection is not always achievable and focus on progress rather than perfection.
- **Practice Flexibility**: Be flexible and adaptable in managing work and personal responsibilities.

Benefits of Work-Life Balance

1. **Improved Health and Well-Being**

Achieving work-life balance contributes to better physical and mental health, reducing stress and preventing burnout.

- **Physical Health**: Maintain physical health through regular exercise, healthy eating, and adequate rest.
- **Mental Health**: Support mental well-being through relaxation, hobbies, and self-care.

2. **Enhanced Job Satisfaction**

   A balanced approach to work and personal life leads to greater job satisfaction and motivation.

   - **Increased Engagement**: Experience higher levels of engagement and satisfaction in your work.
   - **Reduced Turnover**: Reduce the likelihood of job turnover by maintaining a healthy balance.

3. **Stronger Relationships**

   Balancing work and personal life strengthens relationships with family and friends, enhancing overall quality of life.

   - **Quality Time**: Spend meaningful time with loved ones, improving relationship quality and support.
   - **Better Communication**: Foster open communication and understanding in personal relationships.

4. **Increased Productivity**

   A balanced approach to work and personal life enhances productivity and effectiveness in both areas.

   - **Focused Efforts**: Concentrate on work tasks during work hours and personal activities during personal time.
   - **Improved Efficiency**: Achieve better results by managing time and energy effectively.

Achieving work-life balance is essential for maintaining overall well-being, enhancing productivity, and leading a fulfilling life. By setting clear boundaries, prioritizing tasks, practicing self-care, and managing stress, you can create a sustainable balance between work and personal responsibilities. Overcoming common challenges and understanding the benefits of work-life balance will help you lead a more harmonious and rewarding life. Embrace the principles and strategies outlined in this chapter to achieve a healthy and fulfilling work-life balance.

Conclusion

As we conclude our journey through "Time Management Mastery: Powerful Methods to Conquer Procrastination and Enhance Productivity," it's clear that mastering time management is not just about organizing tasks—it's about reshaping how you approach life and work. The strategies and techniques discussed throughout this book are designed to empower you to take control of your time, overcome procrastination, and achieve your fullest potential.

Key Takeaways

1. **Understanding Procrastination**: Recognizing the root causes of procrastination is the first step in overcoming it. By addressing these underlying factors, you can develop more effective strategies to stay on track and remain motivated.
2. **Time Management Techniques**: Implementing proven time management techniques, such as prioritizing tasks, setting clear goals, and using tools like time blocking and the Pomodoro Technique, can significantly enhance your productivity and efficiency.
3. **Productivity Hacks**: Leveraging productivity hacks, including optimizing your workspace, minimizing distractions, and practicing effective delegation, can help you make the most of your time and resources.
4. **Balancing Work and Life**: Achieving work-life balance is crucial for maintaining overall well-being. By setting boundaries, prioritizing self-care, and managing stress, you can create a more harmonious and fulfilling life.
5. **Building Resilience and Maintaining Motivation**: Developing resilience and finding ways to maintain motivation are essential for sustaining productivity and overcoming setbacks. Embrace challenges as opportunities for growth and remain focused on your long-term goals.

Moving Forward

Implementing these strategies is not a one-time effort but a continuous journey. The key to time management mastery lies in persistence and adaptability. As you apply these methods, you may encounter new challenges and opportunities, and it's important to remain flexible and open to adjustments.

1. **Embrace Continuous Improvement**: Regularly assess and refine your time management practices. Seek feedback, track your progress, and make adjustments as needed to stay aligned with your goals.
2. **Stay Committed**: Cultivate a commitment to your personal and professional development. Consistent effort and dedication will yield significant improvements in your productivity and overall effectiveness.
3. **Celebrate Successes**: Acknowledge and celebrate your achievements along the way. Recognizing your progress will reinforce positive habits and keep you motivated.

Final Thoughts

Mastering time management is a transformative process that empowers you to take control of your life and achieve your goals. By conquering procrastination and enhancing productivity, you can unlock new levels of success, satisfaction, and fulfillment.

Thank you for embarking on this journey with "Time Management Mastery." Remember, the tools and strategies shared in this book are not just techniques—they are a pathway to a more productive, balanced, and rewarding life. Embrace the principles, take action, and watch as you transform your approach to time and productivity.

Here's to your continued success and mastery of time management!

www.ingramcontent.com/pod-product-compliance
Lightning Source LLC
Chambersburg PA
CBHW072054230526
45479CB00010B/1056